The Coolest Pets

Birds

Anne O'Daly

KidHaven PUBLISHING

Published in 2024 by
KidHaven Publishing, an Imprint of Greenhaven Publishing, LLC
2544 Clinton St., Buffalo, NY 14224

Portions of this work were originally authored by Dawn Titmus and published as *Birds*.
All new material this edition authored by Anne O'Daly.

Design Manager: Keith Davis
Picture Manager: Sophie Mortimer

Photo Credits:
Front cover: Shutterstock: Butterfly Hunter bl, cynoclub tl, tr, photomaster br.
Interior: Alamy: Juniors Bildarchiv GmbH 23b; Dreamstime: cynoclub 22-23; iStock: Brosa 14, CasPhotography 25b, GloballP 4–5, Leopardinatree 19b, Lusyaya 21b, Multiart 6–7, Nickbeer 12t, pchoul 18t, Emilija Randjelovic 25t, tucko019 7cl, 7cr, vitalssss 8, vitcom 10, Yobra10 15t; Shutterstock: BestPhotoStudio 15b, Butterfly Hunter 26, Coldmoon Photoproject 11t, cynoclub 20–21, GaevoyB 23t, Glass and Nature 29l, guentermanaus 29t, Eric Isselee 1, 12–13, 24, Anna Kaewkkhammul 29b, Kolonko 20, 22, 24, 26, Light Field Studios 7b, Wang LiQiang 27b, Lucky Business 17b, Tanya Morozz 12b, nattanan726 19t, photomaster 17, sabujbd 13, Saman527 9t, santypan 16, Theodore Scott 27t, Elena Shutlova 9b, soririnaja 11b, travelarium.ph 7cl, Santhosh Varghese 5, 21t, Olga Vasilyeva 4, Paul S. Wolf 18t, Daniel Zuppinger 18t.
Key: t=top, b=bottom, c=centre, l=left, r=right

Cataloging-in-Publication Data

Names: O'Daly, Anne
Title: Birds / Anne O'Daly.
Description: Buffalo, New York : Kidhaven Publishing, 2024. |
Series: The coolest pets| Includes index and glossary
Identifiers: ISBN 9781534545472 (pbk) | ISBN 9781534545489 (library bound) | ISBN 9781534545496 (ebook)
Subjects: LCSH: Birds-- Juvenile literature | Birds as pets --Juvenile literature | Pets--Juvenile literature
Classification: LCC SF461.35 O33 2024 | DDC 636.6--dc23

Manufactured in the United States of America

CPSIA compliance information: Batch #CSKH24: For further information contact Greenhaven Publishing LLC at 1-844-317-7404.

Please visit our website, www.greenhavenpublishing.com.
For a free color catalog of all our high-quality books, call toll free 1-844-317-7404 or fax 1-844-317-7405.

Find us on

Contents

Choosing a Bird

A feathered pet can make a fascinating addition to your family. Birds are great fun, but choose your pet carefully. All birds need care and attention, and some are more demanding than others.

Home and Lifestyle

Before you choose a bird, think about how much time and space you have. Parrots like attention. Canaries are happy to be left alone in their cage. Some birds need more space than others. A small bird such as a parakeet is a good choice for an apartment. A larger bird such as a macaw needs a big cage and time to fly outside it. The cage must have enough space for your pet to move around easily.

Healthy Bird

It is important to choose a healthy bird. Your bird should have bright, clear eyes and no bald patches in the feathers. Pet birds need yearly checkups at the vet.

Checklist

- Do you have time to look after a bird?
- Do you have the space for a bird and its cage?
- Are you able to provide your bird with food and water every day?
- Can you make your home a safe place for a bird?
- Will you take your bird to the vet regularly?
- Do you have other pets such as a dog or cat?

Adopt a Bird

Before you buy a bird, see if you can adopt one from your local animal shelter or an avian rescue organization. Avian vets, who specialize in birds, often know of birds in need of homes. You could also check the advertisements in the local paper or pet store.

Next Steps

Birds are great pets, but it is important to choose the right one. This book will help you pick and care for your pet. Learn about four types of birds that are popular as pets. Try your hand at making tasty bird treats. You will also find some fascinating facts about our feathery friends!

Getting Started

Before you bring your pet home, you'll need some basic items. The biggest and most important is the cage. Your pet will also need food and water containers, a birdbath, and some toys.

Playtime

Giving your bird toys to play with will help prevent boredom. Change the toys in the cage frequently for more variety. Try toys that your bird can use for foraging or shredding. You can find these in pet stores or you can make your own. Your bird will also enjoy a birdbath that can be clipped on to the side of the cage.

Checklist

- The biggest cage you can afford.
- Perches for the cage.
- Food and water containers.
- Toys such as ladders and puzzles.
- Birdbath.
- Bird-safe cleaner.

Toys keep birds entertained.

Perches

Perches encourage your bird to exercise. Changing the position of the perches in the cage makes life more interesting for your pet. You can use well-scrubbed branches to make your own perches from non-poisonous trees such as sycamore and apple.

Food and Water

Most cages have covered food and water containers that clip to the side of the cage. Your bird may bathe or leave droppings in an open water container. Most cages have a floor that slides out for easy cleaning. Remove food and droppings from the floor every day.

Food container

Water container

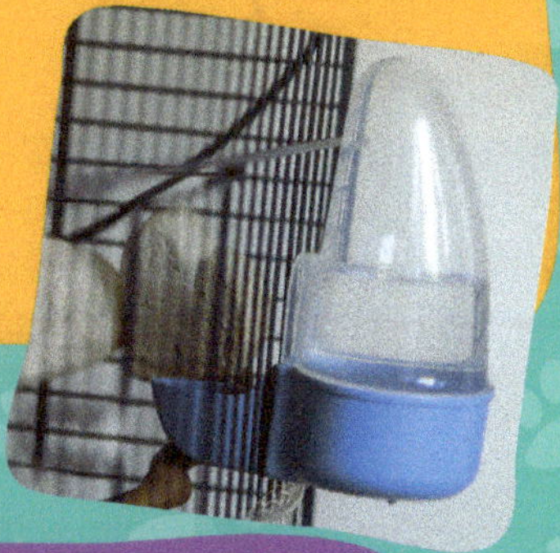

The Cage

Decide where in the home you want the bird to live. It is best not to put a cage in the kitchen as cooking fumes could harm your pet. Keep the cage away from windows, too. The sun could cause your bird to overheat. The best place is next to a wall in a room where you spend a lot of time.

Food and Drink

Food is an important part of caring for your pet. Your bird needs the right type of food, and the right amount, to stay healthy. It also needs a supply of clean water.

Bird Food

Feed your bird a balanced diet with good-quality pellets (dried food) and a variety of fresh fruits, vegetables, and grains. Birdseed does not contain all the nutrients a bird needs, but it is a good snack. Make sure you get the right mix for your bird. Millet sprays are nutritious. Cuttlebones provide calcium. Chewing on them helps birds keep their beak in shape.

Egg Food

Egg food is full of protein and vitamins that your bird needs. You can buy it from the pet supply store. Or you can make your own with hardboiled egg yolks and chopped-up dandelion leaves.

Foods to Avoid

There are some foods that are harmful to birds. Dairy products such as milk and cheese can cause an upset stomach. Foods such as chocolate, avocado, rhubarb leaves, and onions can make birds sick.

Treats and Tidbits

Green leafy vegetables, such as mustard greens, chard, and spinach, can be added to your pet's diet. Most birds also like bell peppers, corn (right), and carrots, and fruits such as banana, melon, and grapes. Make sure the fruit and vegetables are washed and cut into small pieces before feeding them to your pet.

Millet spray

Dandelion

Wild Plants

Parrots and finches eat wild plants such as chickweed and dandelion. If these grow in your yard, make sure they haven't been sprayed with chemicals before giving them to your pet.

Cleaning and Grooming

Birds don't need as much grooming as some other pets. They do most of it themselves. But they still need some help, especially with their claws and beaks. You'll also need to keep their cage clean.

Taking a Bath

Many birds will use a birdbath to keep themselves clean. Some parrots like a fine water spray. A houseplant sprayer is good for this. Fill it with clean, tepid water. Hold it up and away from the bird so the spray falls onto it from above like fine raindrops. Do not spray directly into the bird's face.

Preening

Birds use their beak to comb their feathers. This keeps them clean and removes parasites. Birds also arrange the strands of their feathers so they are lying flat. Birds preen themselves like this several times a day.

Claws and Beaks

In the wild, a bird's claws wear down naturally. A caged bird may have overgrown claws that need to be trimmed. Claws have a blood supply, so it is important to cut off only the sharp, pointed tip. Beaks may also need to be trimmed, particularly in parakeets. It is best to ask the vet to trim the claws and beak.

A Clean Cage

Clean your bird's cage, toys, and containers regularly. This will help keep your pet healthy. Be sure to use a cleaning product that is bird safe—some can harm birds. After cleaning, rinse everything in clean water.

Exercise

Birds like to fly! If there is little space for your bird to fly in its cage, let it spend some time outside the cage. Make sure your home is bird proof first.

Perching

Your bird will want to perch on things when it is out of the cage. Make sure some furniture in the room is suitable for perching. A special bird T-stand (stand in the shape of a T) is ideal.

Settling In

Allow your bird to settle in for a few days when you first bring it home. When it is settled, you can try coaxing it out of its cage. Open the cage door and offer your pet a treat. Allow it to come out at its own pace. Do not try to handle your pet, as it will get scared. Leave the door open so it can come and go when it wants.

Flying Time

The chance for your bird to fly is good exercise and a boredom buster. Close all windows and doors to prevent your bird escaping. Also pull the drapes and close the blinds so your bird does not fly into windows. Make sure any other pets, such as cats and dogs, are safely away in another room. Birds like to chew, so put any wires, cords, or other chewable items out of sight. Turn off any heaters, ceiling fans, and other appliances.

Swing Exercise

Many birds, including parakeets and parrots, enjoy playing on a swing inside their cage. Swinging helps birds get active and healthy. The action makes the feet and leg muscles stronger. It also works the chest muscles and wings.

Training

Many pet birds can be taught to do tricks. Some can be trained to talk! Make sure your bird has plenty of toys, and play with it every day to keep it from getting bored.

Tricks and Treats

Parrots and parakeets are especially good at learning tricks. You could train your bird to turn around, wave, dance, or jump. Use treats as rewards when your bird does what you want it to do.

Ignore Bad Behavior

Ignore the behavior you do not want. Never yell at your bird or punish it. Birds can become aggressive and bite if they are scared. Try distracting your bird from bad behavior. If your bird screams when its food bowls are being filled, give it a toy or snack to keep it busy.

What Did You Say?

Some birds, such as parrots and parakeets, can be taught to talk. Try singing to your bird and copying the sounds it makes. Keep repeating the words you want your bird to say. Keep the training sessions short. A few minutes several times a day is better than a long session. Training a bird to talk takes a lot of patience. Don't be disappointed if your bird doesn't talk back to you immediately!

Finger Tame

Some birds become so tame they will happily sit on your finger. You can encourage your pet to step onto your hand. Carefully place your hand inside the cage alongside the perch. Some birds may find it scary to have a hand in their cage, so go slowly. If your bird steps onto your fingers, reward it with a treat such as a piece of apple.

Keeping Healthy

Birds need the right food and clean water every day to stay healthy. Even so, birds get sick sometimes. Routine trips to the vet will keep your pet healthy and prevent diseases.

Regular Checkups

Take your bird to the vet when you first get it. Also take it once a year for a checkup. Your vet will check your bird's weight and ask questions about your pet's general health. It is best to find a specialist avian vet if you can.

Signs of Illness

A bird can show it is not feeling well in several ways:

* It is not thirsty or hungry.
* It seems tired or less active than usual.
* It sits hunched over, with its feathers fluffed up.
* Its eyes are dull or closed.
* It sleeps on both legs rather than just on one leg.
* It is sneezing or has a runny beak area.
* Its droppings look different from normal.

Take your bird to the vet right away if you think it is ill.

Common Problems

Birds can develop problems with their claws, beak, and feathers. Claws can get too long and make perching difficult. The beak may also grow too long. Birds use their beak for grooming, eating, and balance. An overlong beak can make these behaviors difficult. The vet can help with claw and beak trimmings. Birds may pluck their feathers. There are many reasons for feather plucking, such as sickness, boredom, or a poor diet. Take your bird to the vet for advice if it starts to pluck out its feathers.

Keeping Clean

If your bird has been ill, it's important to clean the cage and food and water containers to prevent disease from spreading. Also be sure to wash your hands every time you handle a sick bird.

Wild Birds

Most pet birds are bred in captivity. They often show the same behavior as birds in the wild. Finches, parrots, and softbills such as toucans are among the most popular birds to keep as pets.

Feeding Habits

Birds in the wild eat food that keeps them fit and healthy. For example, toucans eat mainly fruit. It is important to feed your bird the type of food it would find and eat in the wild.

Singing Birds

In the wild, many birds defend their territory and attract a mate by singing. People keep canaries and singing finches because of their beautiful song.

Flocking Together

Parrots are social birds. In the wild, many types search for food in large flocks and sleep at night in large roosts. If you have a parrot or parakeet as a pet, give it foraging toys and puzzle toys to keep it entertained. Spend as much time as you can talking to and playing with your parrot.

Finding a Mate

Many types of parrots mate for life. Both parents look after the eggs until they hatch and care for the young birds. In finches, only the female bird looks after the eggs and young birds. Some birds, such as lovebirds, are happier as pets if they have a companion to live with. Pairs of lovebirds will play with and groom one another.

Parakeet

The parakeet comes in a variety of colors, from green and blue to white and yellow. Parakeets are some of the most popular pet birds in the world.

Where in the World?

The parakeet comes from Australia. In the wild, the birds fly around in large flocks. In 1840, the English explorer John Gould took a pair of parakeets back to England for breeding. Over time, different color types appeared.

The parakeet is usually active and sociable.

Pet Care

The parakeet does not need a very large cage. It is a good pet bird for people who live in an apartment.

- It feeds on a special parakeet seed mix and leafy greens. It also likes carrots and apples.
- Parakeets need exercise outside the cage, but may be reluctant to return!

Profile

The budgie is a type of parakeet, a member of the parrot family. It grows to about 7 inches (18 cm) long. Budgies are mostly apple green and yellow with a bluish tail in the wild. There are many other color varieties in captive birds. The budgie is a good mimic and can be taught to talk. Pet budgies live for 7 to 10 years.

African Grey Parrot

The African grey parrot is a favorite pet. Highly intelligent and sociable, it is one of the best talkers in the parrot family.

Where in the World?

There are two forms of the African grey—the Congo and the Timneh. The Congo is found across Central Africa, from the west coast to Tanzania and Kenya in the east. The slightly smaller Timneh comes from Ivory Coast and Guinea in West Africa.

The African grey is a smart bird.

Pet Care

African greys are very smart and need lots of activity to stop them from getting bored. Foraging and puzzle toys are good.

- They are curious birds and need plenty of time outside the cage.
- They need a complete pellet diet or seed-based mix, as well as fruit, leafy greens, and vegetables.

Profile

African greys grow 11 to 13 inches (28 to 33 cm) in length. They have grey plumage with bright red or maroon feathers on the tail. Adults have yellow eyes. Young birds have grey eyes. The African grey is one of the best talkers. It learns new words quickly. These birds can live for 50 to 70 years in captivity.

Canary

Canaries come in a wide range of colors. Some types have frilled plumage. They are well known for their ability to sing.

Where in the World?

Canaries come from the Canary Islands, off the northwest coast of Africa. They also live on the Azores and the island of Madeira. The first canaries were taken to Europe in the 1500s. They became popular for their beautiful singing.

The canary is a good pet for people who live in an apartment.

Pet Care

Canaries are cheerful, active birds. They like company and are best kept in pairs.

- Put sand sheets or bird sand at the bottom of the cage to help the canaries digest their food.
- They need a special canary seed mixture, leafy greens, and fruit.

Profile

The canary is a member of the finch family. It grows 4.5 to 8 inches (11.5 to 20 cm) long. In the wild, the canary is a dull brownish green. Domestic canaries vary in color from white and yellow to bright red and orange. Canaries can live for 8 to 10 years.

Zebra Finch

The zebra finch is easy to care for and is an ideal beginner's pet. It is one of the most popular finches. Zebra finches don't like to live alone.

Where in the World?

Zebra finches live wild in Australia and on some Indonesian islands. The first Europeans in Australia described the birds in 1805. Zebra finches were first bred in captivity in Europe from the middle of the 1800s.

The zebra finch is a friendly bird but is unlikely to be finger tame.

Pet Care

The zebra finch is a very sociable bird and should be kept in pairs or groups.

* It needs a large cage with plenty of space for perching.
* It needs a birdbath at least once a week.

Profile

The zebra finch grows up to 4 inches (10 cm) in length. Females are greyish brown with an orange beak. Males have black-and-white bands on the throat, brown patches with white spots on the body, and orange cheek patches. They can live for 5 to 8 years.

Easy-to-Make

Oatmeal Cookies

Make these delicious healthy oatmeal treats for your bird. Most birds will love them.

You Will Need:

* 1 cup (90 g) dry oatmeal
* 1 egg
* Small amount of crumbled eggshell (optional)
* 2 to 3 tablespoons honey
* Vegetable oil for greasing

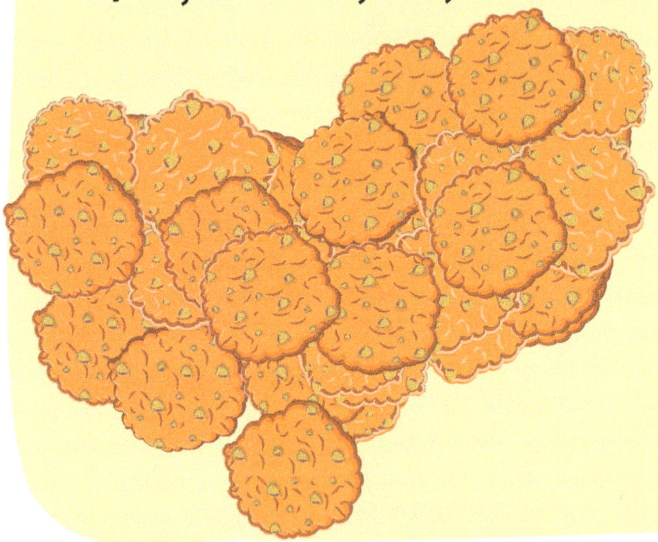

1 Ask an adult to preheat the oven to 350°F (180°C).

2 Mix the oatmeal and egg together in a bowl.

3 Add a little of the eggshell if using, for extra calcium.

4 Add 2 to 3 tablespoons of honey.

5 Grease a cookie sheet with a little vegetable oil.

6 Spread the oatmeal mixture onto the cookie sheet.

7 Bake the mixture in the oven for 8 to 10 minutes, or until it is firm. Ask an adult to take it out.

8 Allow to cool, then cut the mixture into small, bite-sized treats.

You can keep any uneaten treats in the fridge for up to three days.

Fun Facts

Hummingbirds can hover, fly forward, and fly backward. They beat their wings about 80 times per second.

People have used domestic homing pigeons to carry messages for thousands of years. They can find their way home over extremely long distances.

Puck, a pale blue male parakeet, knew 1,728 words. Puck even made up his own phrases. He died in 1994, but he still holds the world record for having the largest vocabulary of any bird.

Some birds are so smart they can make and use tools. Crows, for example, use sticks to reach insects in tree bark.

Scientists believe birds developed from therapods, a group of small dinosaurs. The feet of therapods resemble those of bird feet.

There are about 10,000 recognized bird species in the world. About 13 percent are endangered.

A person who studies the behavior and habitat of birds is called an ornithologist.

The Christmas Island frigatebird has a wingspan of about 7 feet (2.1 m). It can stay in the air for a week without resting.

Owls can rotate their heads up to 270 degrees without injuring themselves.

Glossary

avian relating to birds.

aviary enclosure where birds are kept, usually with space for them to fly.

breed (1) to take care of a group of animals to produce more animals of a particular kind. (2) a particular kind of animal that has been produced by breeding.

calcium substance that animals and people need for strong, healthy bones.

captivity the state of being kept in a cage.

cuttlebone bone from a cuttlefish, made of light, chalky material.

domestic living with people.

flock group of birds.

foraging searching for something such as food.

millet type of grass seed used for food.

mimic copy someone's behavior or speech.

nutrient substance that animals and people need to live and grow.

parakeet small parrot.

parasite an animal that lives in or on another animal and gets food from it.

plumage feathers covering a bird's body.

preen use the beak to clean and arrange feathers.

protein substance in some foods that animals and people need to live and grow.

roost place where birds rest or sleep.

softbill type of bird that has a bill suited to feeding on soft foods, such as fruit.

territory an area of land that an animal lives in and defends.

Further Resources

Books

Greenwood, Nancy. *My Pet Parakeet.* Buffalo, NY: Gareth Stevens Publishing, 2023.

Morris, Harold. *Crazy About Birds.* New York, NY: Crabtree Publishing, 2022.

Rossiter, Brienna. *My Pet Bird.* Mendota Heights, MN: Little Blue Readers, 2023.

Websites

Audubon for Kids!
www.audubon.org/get-outside/activities/audubon-for-kids
It's never too early to start birding. Explore this hobby with the National Audubon Society.

Birds
kids.nationalgeographic.com/animals/birds
Learn more about birds with National Geographic Kids.

The Best Pet Birds for Kids
be.chewy.com/the-best-pet-birds-for-kids/
Explore these pet bird options with your parents or caregivers before choosing your bird.

Publisher's note to parents and teachers: Our editors have reviewed the websites listed here to make sure they're suitable for students. However, websites may change frequently. Please note that students should always be supervised when they access the internet.

Index